How to Be a Christmas Angel

Scott Matthews
and Barbara Alpert

P

PINNACLE BOOKS

To our special angels:
Skyler (from Uncle Scott)

Lauren, Stephanie,
and Charlie (from Aunt Barbara)

PINNACLE BOOKS are published by

Kensington Publishing Corp.
850 Third Avenue
New York, NY 10022

First Printing: November, 1995
ISBN: 0-7860-0199-2
Printed in the United States of America

*I*n this season of miraculous birth, celebrate every child—especially your own.

✳

*O*ffer your arm to elderly neighbors caught in the holiday rush.

✳

*P*olish your halo with a secret good deed.

✳

*P*lay volunteer Santa in a children's ward, and tell stories of the wonder of Christmas.

*O*rganize a "Christmas-dinner" canned goods drive in your office.

✳

*D*eliver Christmas baskets in person to needy families.

✳

*G*ather the children on your block to go Christmas caroling.

✳

*D*onate your caroling dollars to your Salvation Army shelter.

*

*B*ake gingerbread snowmen for a nearby kindergarten class.

*

*S*hare your good health with others—donate a pint of blood during the holidays.

*

String cranberries and popcorn for older neighbors with less nimble fingers.

＊

Make a holiday gift to remember by putting family photos in beautiful scrapbooks.

＊

Head a "Donate-Your-Favorite-Christmas-Book" drive at a local school library.

＊

*H*ang a wreath of holly and pine branches on a neighbor's unadorned door.

✷

*B*ake Christmas tree cookies for the local blood bank's holiday drive.

✷

*M*ake your Christmas tree a "family tree" by framing small photos as ornaments.

✷

*V*olunteer to make a first Christmas happier by holding premies in a hospital.

✳

*O*rganize a Christmas parade in your neighborhood, with kids and pets in costume.

✳

*T*hrow a joint Hanukkah, Christmas, and Kwanzaa party to celebrate with all faiths.

✳

ℛent Christmas classic videos and deliver them to people who can't get out.

✳

𝒮pend Christmas Eve delivering holiday meals to AIDS patients.

✳

𝒞haperone a group of children to the caroling service at Midnight Mass.

✳

*O*rganize a coat drive and persuade neighbors and friends to empty their closets.

✳

*S*pend a part of Christmas Day at a nursing home, visiting those who are alone.

✳

*T*each your kids the true meaning of Christmas by having them donate a favorite toy.

✳

*O*rganize an "Orphans" Christmas dinner, and invite all the unattached people you know.

＊

*M*ake an audiotape of Christmas carols to send to a serviceman overseas.

＊

*M*ake a video of your family Christmas for relatives who can't attend.

＊

*S*ave your Christmas cards to make into ornaments for next year's gifts.

✳

*O*ffer to help decorate your church for the holidays.

✳

*V*olunteer to read "Twas the Night Before Christmas" to blind children.

✳

*H*old doors for everyone overwhelmed with Christmas packages—and offer to help.

Organize a group of parents to deck the halls of your children's school.

✳

Give pairs of gloves to everyone with outstretched hands in this season of warmth.

✳

When the family gathers for the holidays, create a family genealogy.

✳

*P*repare double recipes of your holiday dishes for the family of a hospitalized friend.

*

*S*et aside a family Saturday to make panettone (Italian Christmas bread) from scratch.

*

*T*ake this holy season to remind the people who mean a lot to you just how much they do.

*

*O*pen your heart to others now and in the New Year.

*H*ave family members take turns telling the story of Christmas in front of the fire.

✳

*W*hen someone you love says, "I wish . . . ," make their Christmas dream come true.

✳

*R*ecycle your Christmas tree.

✳

*R*aise your voice in holiday song or for a good cause.

$\mathcal{D}$o something for someone else every day during December.

✳

$\mathcal{M}$ake a wish for peace on the star of wonder.

✳

$\mathcal{S}$hare your love of the season by visiting an animal shelter to choose your new pet.

✳

$\mathcal{T}$ake kids to an open field and make snow angels as far as the eye can see.

*F*ind a bright star in the sky and name it after someone you've loved and lost.

✳

*G*et an early start on your Christmas letter so it's in the mail *before* the year ends.

✳

*H*elp children practice reading aloud by reading holiday stories into a tape recorder.

✳

*M*ake your hearth a welcome mat for Santa.

*P*ray for peace at Christmas with millions all over the world.

✳

*B*e as generous with time and money as you can this holiday season.

✳

*P*ractice compassion in this time of spiritual rebirth.

✳

*S*end holiday postcards this year, and donate what you save on postage to charity.

$\mathcal{R}$eflect on how God has blessed you and those you love.

✳

$\mathcal{G}$ive the gift of hope to all you meet.

✳

$\mathcal{A}$nswer a child's letter to Santa—and let your gifts arrive anonymously.

✳

$\mathcal{A}$dopt a needy family through a local church, and make it a Christmas to remember.

Transform your town for Christmas by decorating windows with spray-on snow.

*

Encourage vacationing college kids to devote a day or two to helping others.

*

Apologize to anyone you wronged during the year.

*

Feed the birds and enjoy their song of thanks.

Read one book during the holidays that affirms your faith.

*

Help kids decorate a Christmas jar to fill with pennies all year for their favorite charity.

*

Clean out your linen closet and donate your best old stuff to Goodwill.

*

Give whenever you're asked this holiday season.

*A*stonish strangers by paying bus fare when they're burdened with kids and packages.

✳

*O*rganize a carpool to save on gas and cut down on holiday traffic.

✳

*M*ake spirits bright and the midnight clear by collecting eyeglasses for New Eyes for the Needy.

✳

Remember Christ our Savior was born on Christmas Day.

✳

After you buy your Christmas tree, plant a tree somewhere for a future Christmas.

✳

Ask a nursing home if you can be a Christmas "buddy" to a lonely senior.

✳

*T*each your children pride in their ancestors' holiday customs.

✳

*R*ecycle your tinsel this year and use rechargeable batteries in Christmas toys.

✳

*W*atch fewer games on TV during the holidays and play more with your kids.

✳

$\mathcal{V}$isit local museums to see how Christmas is celebrated in the past and around the world.

✳

$\mathcal{T}$ry to do better between now and next Christmas.

✳

$\mathcal{S}$tart saving your annual Christmas letters to create a family holiday history.

✳

$\mathcal{R}$emember as you prepare your own holiday feast to count your blessings.

*O*ffer festive non-alcoholic beverages at your parties so those you love will be safer.

✳

*S*ing your heart out at Midnight Mass.

✳

*I*nvite friends who don't observe Christmas to share one of your festive events.

✳

*L*earn how other religious groups celebrate during this time of peace and joy.

*W*rite a letter to the editor praising your town's Christmas spirit.

✳

*I*f you don't own a Nativity scene, make the creation of one a family crafts project.

✳

*S*end Christmas cards that benefit a charity or donate some profits to a good cause.

✳

*R*ecord Christmas memories by taking lots of photographs.

✳

*C*elebrate your family's closeness by joining hands before Christmas dinner.

✳

*M*ake a joyful noise when you praise the Lord.

✳

*G*o home for the holidays if you can.

✳

Share the joy of opening presents with faraway family by passing the phone around.

*

Find the holiness in everyday life during Christmas and sustain it in the coming months.

*

In this joyful season, give the kiss of peace to friends you meet.

*

*I*nvite a stranger to share your pew at Midnight Mass.

✳

*G*ive the gift of saying "I love you" this Christmas to someone who hasn't heard it enough.

✳

*P*ractice kindness as you race through your holiday preparations.

✳

*H*ave plenty of carrot sticks and sparkling water available for Christmas guests watching their weight.

✳

*D*on't be a Scrooge.

✳

*D*raw your family close around you at this beautiful time.

✳

*S*end cards signed "Love, Santa" to nursing home residents who don't get much mail.

Run Christmas errands for an elderly person who has trouble getting around.

✳

Give thanks.

✳

Believe in what you cannot see.

✳

Bring tidings of comfort and joy to all you meet.

✳

*S*hare stories with your kids of favorite Christmas mornings when you were a child.

✳

*P*rovide scrumptious holiday treats that preserve your loved ones' health.

✳

*S*hare your Christmas meal.

✳

*H*ave your children find the Star of Bethlehem and describe what it means to them.

*L*et good cheer begin with you at Christmas.

✳

*J*oin the choir at your church so you can sing at Midnight Mass.

✳

*D*ance with a shy coworker at your company Christmas party.

✳

*S*how your faith in all you do this holiday season.

✳

Do your best to give others a very merry Christmas.

✳

Don't recycle fruitcake.

✳

Pray hard for a white Christmas.

✳

Look for miracles in every child's eyes.

✳

Give the gift of giving.

Create a new family ritual that reflects the true spirit of Christmas.

✳

Donate red stocking caps to a hospital nursery for the first Christmas babies of the year.

✳

Give someone you love the nearest thing to gold, frankincense, and myrrh.

✳

Write a new family verse to "Jingle Bells."

Put candles in every window to light Santa's way in the darkness.

✻

Give all the single women you know corsages of mistletoe to bring them luck.

✻

Celebrate all twelve days of Christmas.

✻

Resolve before New Year's that this year you'll give more than you take.

*W*rite a Christmas letter to thank the one person who made you believe in yourself.

*

*M*ake a list of twelve goals you want to accomplish by next Christmas, and begin.

*

*W*hen your spouse gets home from Christmas shopping, give him or her the best back rub you can.

*

Toss all your regrets and "Bah Humbugs" into the fireplace as the Yule Log burns.

✳

Give your household helpers a "thank-you" card along with their holiday gifts.

✳

Put visions of sugarplums in your childrens' heads.

✳

*M*ake peace with your parents in time for Christmas.

*

*L*isten faithfully to your angel's voice as you prepare to celebrate the Savior's birth.

*

*E*nlist the littlest angels to make Christmas bright all through the neighborhood.

*

*M*ake time during the holidays to strengthen family ties.

*

*W*ear red.

*

*M*ake a pilgrimage to Bethlehem in your heart.

*

*T*ake a homebound neighbor to see the holiday lights downtown.

*

*L*eave holiday leftovers in a bowl on your porch for the neighborhood stray cat.

❋

*G*ive all those around you the gift of your kind disposition.

❋

*S*pread your angel's wings as you make Christmas charity donations in a friend's name.

❋

Practice understanding when bumped by harried holiday shoppers.

✳

Pin a sprig of holly to each guest's jacket as people arrive for Christmas dinner.

✳

Learn all the verses of your favorite carols, and lead friends and family in song.

✳

*W*ear one red and one green sock, just to bring a smile to someone's face.

*

*T*ie bells to children's sneakers, and invite them to dance for joy.

*

*P*oint out to others the beauty of Christmas that surrounds us all.

*

Give your place on line to someone who looks like she's shopped till she dropped.

*

Babysit your friends' kids so they can go Christmas shopping.

*

Cover your Christmas cards and packages with Christmas seals.

*

*H*elp your loved ones learn to fly higher than Santa's sleigh.

*

*T*each your children to write thank-you notes that express their joy.

*

*L*ift someone's spirits with a hearty "Ho-ho-ho!"

*

*T*reat a child to a one-horse open sleigh ride.

*

*H*elp a friend find his way by the light of the North Star.

✳

*G*ive a Grinch a reason to believe in Christmas.

✳

*M*ake time to play in the snow with your kids, or a neighbor's.

✳

*K*eep spirits bright around you.

✳

*V*olunteer to direct the Sunday School Christmas pageant.

*

*T*ake an elderly neighbor Christmas shopping and out to lunch.

*

*L*et nothing you dismay.

*

Teach reading to adults so next year they'll be able to read "Twas the Night Before Christmas" to their own kids.

＊

Share the tradition of an American Christmas with a newly arrived immigrant.

＊

Join with your children's teacher to create a class Christmas project for the community.

＊

*E*ven if you have no children in a class, volunteer to help with school holiday preparations.

✳

*H*elp someone who needs transportation visit department store holiday windows.

✳

*H*ang an ornament on your tree to honor a friend who passed away this year.

✳

*S*uggest that your town create a living Nativity scene for a few nights before Christmas.

✳

*H*ave hot chocolate on hand in case Christmas carolers drop by.

✳

*B*ring your pets to be blessed at your local church.

✳

*R*emind people about the hazards to children and pets of eating poinsettias and holly.

$\mathcal{P}$ut on a red nose and pull a child's sled across a snowy field.

*

$\mathcal{G}$ive a gift to those who make your life run smoothly.

*

$\mathcal{D}$on't forget to wish teachers and storekeepers a Merry Christmas.

*

Keep a list of ways you can make the holidays brighter and check off one a day.

✳

Offer to push another person's car out of a snowbank or off a slick hill.

✳

Carve the words "Merry Christmas" across your neighbor's snowy lawn.

✳

*P*ledge a dollar to charity for each point scored by your local team in December.

✳

*S*ay grace before eating Christmas dinner.

✳

*S*urprise a fellow Christmas shopper by giving up a closer parking space to the car behind you.

✳

*B*uy a cup of coffee for someone working out in the cold.

*L*isten closely when people share their Christmas memories.

❋

*W*hen neighbors go away for the holidays, offer to take in their papers and mail.

❋

*C*reate your own gift cards with hand-lettered messages of peace and joy.

❋

*M*ake a stranger's day by smiling and saying, "Merry Christmas."

✳

*H*eal old wounds by inviting someone you haven't seen in ages to share Christmas eggnog.

✳

*S*pread Christmas joy everywhere you go.

✳

*G*ive from your heart.

✳

*H*elp sinners to be reconciled with the Lord.

✻

*L*earn to say "Merry Christmas" in many different languages.

✻

*D*are someone you love who's a bit conservative to wear a colorful Christmas tie.

✻

*S*hare your grandparents with friends who live far from their own.

*T*each a child to turn a corrugated box into a sled, and spend a day on a hill.

✳

*C*reate your own "Miracle on 34th Street" by proving to a child that Santa is real.

✳

*T*ake a "Scrooge-y" friend to see a local production of *A Christmas Carol*.

✳

*H*um Christmas carols in the elevator and see who joins in.

✳

*G*ive the gift of time at Christmas to new parents by babysitting.

✳

*T*ake a retired friend out to a pre-Christmas lunch and catch up on old times.

✳

*M*ake a donation in Santa's name to the local "Neediest Cases" campaign.

✳

*F*orgive someone's debt this Christmas.

✳

*M*ake it a family project to adopt a child through a relief organization.

✳

*B*ake homemade dog and cat treats for a local animal shelter.

*D*on't wait to be asked to help when friends have the holiday blues—just show up.

✳

*H*elp hospice patients send holiday cards to loved ones.

✳

*V*olunteer to answer phones at a crisis hotline during the holidays.

✳

*O*ffer to play Santa for a local daycare center.

*R*emember the school crossing guard who helps your child across icy streets.

❋

*R*ecycle your holiday wrapping paper for next year and save a tree.

❋

*B*uild a Santa Claus snowman for all to enjoy.

❋

*I*nvite your kids' teachers to a holiday gathering to express your appreciation.

Make sure someone at each holiday party is the designated driver, so all get home safely.

✳

Suggest to children that thoughtful homemade gifts are always welcome.

✳

Help a child mail a letter to the North Pole.

✳

Enlist your entire office to answer letters to Santa received by the post office.

*L*isten to the Christmas bells, and remember how angels get their wings.

*

*M*ake tired salesclerks smile with a warm thank you.

*

*W*hen you go home for Christmas, visit a teacher who changed your life.

*

*I*f your family can't be home for Christmas, plan a conference call linking everyone.

＊

*B*orrow a tripod so you can be in the videotape on Christmas morning.

＊

*A*sk Santa what *he* wants for Christmas the next time you sit on his lap.

＊

*G*o a little overboard when celebrating Christmas.

*T*ake a little girl to see *The Nutcracker* for the first time.

✳

*B*ring a basket of Christmas cheer to your local fire and police stations.

✳

*S*urprise your kids by waking up before they do on Christmas morning.

✳

$\mathcal{P}$ay the highway toll for a car behind you, and yell "Merry Christmas."

✳

$\mathcal{B}$e the first one to wish "Happy Holidays!" to everyone you meet.

✳

$\mathcal{M}$aneuver two of your best single friends until they're standing under the mistletoe.

✳

Offer your gifts with no strings attached except for those holding the pretty bows.

✳

Decorate a tiny Christmas tree to brighten the hospital room of a stranger.

✳

Practice forgiveness this holiday season until you get it right.

✳

Shovel the snow from your neighbors' walk before they wake up.

＊

Thank the police officer on the beat for being on duty during the holidays.

＊

Remember Tiny Tim's prayer: "God bless us, every one!"

＊

$\mathcal{H}$elp rekindle someone's faith in the miracle of Christmas.

✳

$\mathcal{C}$elebrate the holidays like the sisters in *Little Women* by sharing all you have.

✳

$\mathcal{D}$on't forget that Christmas is a birthday, after all.

✳

$\mathcal{M}$ake your gifts as wonderfully wise as the Magi.

✳

*H*ug someone who has the Christmas blues.

✳

*B*e a merry soul and a cheerful giver.

✳

*K*eep the holidays holy.

✳

*W*hen you see someone waiting under mistletoe, pucker up.

✳

*J*ust this once, give your dog his own plate of Christmas dinner.

*

*S*uggest that instead of an office grab bag, you send money to the Red Cross.

*

*D*iscover the true pleasure of giving anonymously this season.

*

Show your appreciation by using the gifts people gave you in their presence.

✳

Throw a holiday party where the price of admission is a coat for the needy.

✳

Warm up your spouse's car on cold December days.

✳

*I*nstead of a photocopied Christmas letter, write personal notes to close friends.

✳

*I*nclude the poor in spirit in your Christmas prayers.

✳

*B*e generous with Christmas tips to the kids who deliver your pizza and paper.

✳

*E*nlist your children to write Christmas messages like "Ho-ho-ho" on all the frosty windows.

*B*ring a colorful poinsettia to a neighbor who can't get out during the holidays.

✳

*L*et a child win a snowball fight.

✳

*P*ut the message of the Christmas sermon into practice all year long.

✳

*D*rop off the holiday issues of your favorite magazines at the nearest senior center.

*W*ish every Santa you meet a very merry Christmas.

❋

*O*n Christmas Day, give the gift of life by having all the adults sign organ donor cards.

❋

*M*ake a wish come true for a terminally ill child.

❋

*G*ive copies of your favorite books as Christmas gifts.

❋

$\mathcal{D}$on't let the Christmas spirit evaporate when it's time to toss the tree.

✳

$\mathcal{H}$ave your children write stories about the true meaning of Christmas.

✳

$\mathcal{W}$ith every carol you trumpet, sing as though heavenly angels were listening.

✳

*I*nvite a shaky ice skater to glide alongside your steadier skates.

✳

*W*hen you "buy one, get one free" this Christmas, give the free one away.

✳

*S*ign up now to become a Big Brother or Sister for the holidays and beyond.

✳

*W*hen the going gets tough this season, remember Tiny Tim made it through.

✳

*P*lant a tree in honor of a child born in this holiest of seasons.

✳

*L*et your angels show you the way to help those you love.

✳

*L*ead Christmas caroling at a senior citizens' home.

*T*ake the whole family to a Christmas tree farm to pick out your perfect tree.

✳

*I*f friends are alone for the holidays, invite them to join you.

✳

*S*pread the happiness you feel throughout the holidays.

✳

*B*e good for goodness' sake.

*R*escue a cat from the animal shelter and name her Mrs. Claws.

✳

*L*isten to the prayers of children.

✳

*B*e someone's secret Santa, and fulfill a heart's desire.

✳

*L*oan your copy of *It's a Wonderful Life* to each of your neighbors for a night.

*C*arry the Christmas spirit with you all year long.

✳

*F*ind your faith in the glory of the Christmas story.

✳

*P*lan a family walk on Christmas Day through the nearest "winter wonderland."

✳

*M*ake a special effort to serve everyone's favorites for Christmas dinner.

✳

*H*elp this season be a new beginning for you and your loved ones.

✳

*B*e a Scrooge with your anger.

✳

*T*each your children the satisfaction in service to others.

✳

*S*tart a tradition of saving a chunk of the Christmas tree trunk for next year's Yule Log.

$\mathcal{E}$-mail Christmas greetings to strangers and sign them "Santa."

*

$\mathcal{B}$uy a stuffed reindeer for a stuffy friend who could use a hug.

*

$\mathcal{W}$arm your dearest's heart with a surprise sleigh ride.

*

Sing "Santa Claus Is Coming To Town" to a pouting child.

✳

Challenge a child to find two snowflakes that are alike.

✳

Warm someone's frosty lips with a loving kiss.

✳

Help make the biggest snowman on the block.

✳

Count your blessings, and don't stop until you reach one hundred.

＊

Stop a Grinch from stealing Christmas.

＊

Write "I Love You" on a frosted window.

＊

Wax a child's toboggan for a speedy ride Christmas afternoon.

＊

*I*nspire a young skater to dream of a miracle on ice.

*

*T*hank those who make you realize you have a wonderful life.

*

*I*nstead of tossing snowballs, build castles in the snow.

*

*C*reate magic and miracles on Christmas morning.

*H*old up the littlest child in the room to crown the tree with the star.

✷

*A*waken others in this beautiful season to the presence of angels in their lives.

✷

*W*hen you spot Rudolph's blinking nose in the sky, alert the nearest child.

✷

*G*ive every child on your list a gift certificate for books that tickle the imagination.

✳

*F*ax a Christmas greeting, and make someone's day at work.

✳

*C*all a lonely friend on Christmas Day to say how much you care.

✳

*B*e a friend who listens in this season of fragile emotions.

✳

*P*lay Pollyanna's "Glad Game" at Christmas, and find the good in every thing.

✳

*J*oin with a best buddy to plot a course for a healthy New Year.

✳

𝒦eep the fantasy alive for a child—eat the cookies left for Santa.

✳

ℋelp someone else to give up guilt this year.

✳

𝒯hank your mother for teaching you the glory of Christmas.

✳

*W*ait to place the baby Jesus in your Nativity scene until early Christmas morning.

✸

*I*nvite a child to blaze a path through new-fallen snow.

✸

*R*eflect on the true meaning of Christmas.

✸

*B*ring joy to someone's world.

✸

$\mathcal{D}$eck the halls with family photos of other Christmases.

*

$\mathcal{N}$ever let someone go to bed mad on Christmas Eve.

*

$\mathcal{P}$ull everyone together for a group hug on Christmas morning.

*

*L*et the memories of those you loved and lost this year live on in your heart.

❋

*B*e merry and bright.

❋

*M*ake someone's Christmas the best ever.

❋